MAKING ADS WORK

If you're going to advertise, know how to do it right.
This is how.

The Writings of Roy H. Williams
As compiled by Wizard of Ads® Partner

Craig Arthur

PRESS
Wizard Academy Press™
Buda, Texas

MAKING ADS WORK

Printed in Canada.

Wizard Academy Press™
1760 FM 967
Buda, TX 78610
512.295.5700
800.425.4769
www.WizardAcademyPress.com

Library of Congress Cataloging-in-Publication Data
Arthur, Craig
     Making ads work: if you're going to advertise, know how to do it right. this is how./ Craig Arthur.
          p.   cm.
          ISBN 1-932226-27-3

Ordering Information
To order additional copies, contact your local bookstore,call 800.425.4769, or visit www.WizardAcademyPress.com
Bulk Discount Avalible

A WIZARD OF ADS® GUIDE FOR BUSINESS OWNERS & ADVERTISING PROFESSIONALS

Wizard of Ads® Partners

The United States
Austin, Texas (Home Office)
China Spring, Texas
Dallas, Texas
Oklahoma City, Oklahoma
Phoenix, Arizona
Sidney, Nebraska
Anchorage, Alaska
Orlando, Florida

Canada
Stratford, Ontario
Ottawa, Ontario

Australia
Townsville, Queensland

MAKING ADS WORK

The writings of *Roy H. Williams
As compiled by Wizard of Ads® Partner Craig Arthur

*Roy H. Williams is founder of Williams Marketing, Wizard Academy and the Wizard of Ads® Partners consulting group. Speaker, Teacher, Consultant, and best selling Author of the Wizard of Ads® Trilogy, Free the Beagle Trilogy, Accidental Magic, Thought Particles and the worldwide free weekly newsletter The Monday Morning Memo.

This guide contains a selection of Monday Morning Memos, chapters from The Wizard of Ads® Trilogy, findings from the Wizard Academy Research Group, leading   neuroscientists and university professors, combined with the daily practices of Roy H. Williams, and the Partners of Wizard of Ads®.

CONTRIBUTING AUTHOR
Craig Arthur - Wizard of Ads® Partners. Australia

Relational vs. Transactional Case Study (page 9-10)
Scott Broderick - Wizard of Ads® Partners. Canada East

SPECIAL THANKS

Dave Young for his seminar transcripts
Michele Miller, Garry Watkins, Steve Rae – editing
Sean Taylor for the Cover Design
& for being an all round helpful guy
Princess Pennie, Corrine Taylor, David Stanley
Shelley Brough & Dee Johnson,
Simply Pies Bakery Cafes
Phillip Gould, Cash Converters
Angela

&

Roy H. Williams
For spending twenty-five years studying what makes
people do the things they do and how to make ads work.

CONTENTS

"I have never studied selling.
Too many liars, thieves, and con men have studied selling,
and the world is full of sales trainers.
Instead, I've spent a lifetime studying how to make ads work."

- Roy H. Williams, the Wizard of Ads® -

From where you are in business to where you
want to be, Wizard of Ads will help you
GET THERE.

Wizard of Ads Partners
"Get There"

THE SIMPLE TRUTH IS THAT MOST ADVERTISING ISN'T WORKING LIKE IT SHOULD. BUT WHY NOT?

It's not working because in traditional advertising wisdom, tradition far outweighs wisdom. Advertisers are making decisions based on irrelevant information. This information is then applied using unwritten advertising rules that simply don't work. These rules have never worked, and they never will.

So don't just think "outside" the current box called advertising. Thinking outside still leaves you attached. And you will never see dramatic improvements in your advertising until you **disconnect yourself** altogether. So jump out of your current box and give it a good kick, because it's costing you money. How much exactly? Read on.

Add together all the advertising dollars you invested in the last 12 months. Include radio, TV, newspaper, flyers, yellow pages, brochures, internet, printing costs, and production costs, add it all up. Apply that dollar amount to the steps below.

Step 1
Advertising dollars invested in the last 12 months
$_____ *(Example: $90,000)*

Step 2
What percentage do you feel was wasted or was ineffective?
_____% *(Example: 70%)*

Step 3
Multiply your total ad budget by the above percentage.
$_____ *(Example: $90,000 x .7 = $63,000)*
This will give you the ad dollars you feel were wasted last year

Note: The wastage across all business categories ranges between 50 to 90 percent.

It may make you feel queasy looking at all those wasted dollars, but at least the facts are on the table.

Now, to make any progress understanding how advertising really works and to make your ad dollars perform, I need you to give me a big, blank, white sheet of paper to draw on. **I need you to leave your prejudices, preconceptions, education, assumptions, and your previous way of thinking about advertising at the door.** After you have finished reading this guide, you can then pick them back up and re-integrate them if you wish.

But for now I need that big, blank, piece of paper ... because I am going to teach you how Wizard of Ads® makes clients grow not just by percentages, but by **Multiples!**

Can you give me that big blank sheet?

Good!

Let's go.

"(The Reader) will take from my book what he can bring to it.
The dull witted will get dullness and the brilliant may find things
in my book I didn't even know were there."
- John Steinbeck, 1952 -

THE THREE WORLDS OF BUSINESS

1. The World outside Your Door

Think about the people in your city who don't do business with you: Is it because they don't know about you? Or is it because they do?

The customer's expectations and preconceptions can be found in the World outside Your Door. This is where your reputation lives in the hearts of the people. What is your typical customer's predisposition toward you? What expectations does she have? How well are you really known, and how much of what is known, is real?

The World outside Your Door is where media dominance is established. Will this be accomplished by you or your competitor?

Simply put, the World outside Your Door is the world of advertising, the place where success begins.

But it definitely doesn't end there.

2. The World inside Your Door

The World inside Your Door is the world of the customer's experience: the place where you must make good on all the bold promises you've made in your ads. How well do you deliver on those promises?

Eyes, ears, nose, and skin enter the World inside Your Door. How pleasant are the signals they receive? Regardless of whether your customer steps into a physical store or merely contacts you by phone or internet, advertising is finished the moment that contact is made.

Don't expect advertising to fix problems inside your door. If there's a deficiency in the quality of your customer's experience, fix it!

3. The World of the Executive Office

Earthquakes happen when seismic waves travel outward from an epicenter to literally shake the world. Likewise, businessquakes begin in the office of the business owner and spread from department to department; shaking both paradigm and tradition until the size and shape of the business finally fits the vision of the business owner.

Some businessquakes are the genesis of a brilliant future; others result in bankruptcy. But at the epicenter of every one of them is the chair of the business owner. The quality of decisions made in that chair is ultimately revealed in the long-term profitability of the business.

To understand a business owner's vision, you need only visit the business. Whom to hire, how much to pay, where to be located, hours of operation, product pricing, merchandising, staff training and motivation are all the result of businessquakes in the mind of the business owner. From there, the ever-spreading ripples create the world of the customer's experience, and then continue outward until they are revealed in the company's advertising, forever telling the story that is uniquely and wonderfully their own.

Uncovery – Digging for the Diamond

There is a story that is uniquely and wonderfully your own, but you'll never uncover it by trying to imitate the success of others. When digging for the diamond; that is your own unique story (Your *Sword in the Stone) you'll have to sift through a lot of worthless dirt before you find a single nugget of radiant truth. But in the end, it's worth it.

Don't be discouraged. Dig for the diamond. Find the story that is uniquely and wonderfully your own, then tell that story with every ounce of your being.

WizardSword Vocabulary

- The Sword in the Stone -

The focal idea. The axis upon which all else revolves. The standard you will never compromise. The story that is unique to your business.

TRANSACTIONAL VS. RELATIONAL SHOPPERS

Can't decide what information to include in your ads?
Surprise: There's more than one answer.

Q: What is the most important information to put in an ad: Price? Selection? Quick and friendly service? Store hours? Brands we carry? Guarantees? Testimonials? The fact that we're a family-owned business?

A: Every person has a transactional mode and a relational mode of shopping. And the "right" thing to say can be determined only when you know which mode the shopper is in.

1. **Transactional shoppers** are focused only on today's transaction and give little thought to the possibility of future purchases.
2. Their only fear is of paying more than they had to pay. Transactional shoppers are looking for price and value.
3. They enjoy the process of comparing and negotiating and will likely shop at several stores before making their decision to purchase.
4. Transactional shoppers do their own research so they won't need the help of an expert. Consumer Reports are published primarily for the transactional shopper.
5. Because they enjoy the process, transactional shoppers don't consider their time spent shopping to be part of the purchase price.

1. **Relational shoppers** consider today's transaction to be one in a long series of many future purchases. They are looking less for a product than for a store in which to buy it.
2. Their only fear is of making a poor choice. Relational shoppers will purchase as soon as they have confidence. Will your store and your staff give them this confidence they seek?
3. They don't enjoy the process of shopping and negotiating.
4. Relational shoppers are looking principally for an expert they can trust.
5. They consider their time to be part of the purchase price.
6. Confident that they have found "*the right place to buy*," relational shoppers are very likely to become repeat customers.

As was stated earlier, every person has a transactional mode and a relational mode of shopping, so don't be surprised when you see yourself in both descriptions. You, like all other shoppers, are extremely transactional in certain product and service categories and wholly relational in others. Due to the fact that shoppers in transactional mode will shop all over town and love to negotiate, merchants often wrongfully conclude that most shoppers stay in transactional mode. But in truth, more purchases are quietly made by customers in relational mode.

Here's a simple Transactional vs. Relational case study:

Ten shoppers in total, five of these shoppers are transactional, and the other five are relational. All shoppers want to buy the same product with a recommended retail price of $100.

The transactional shoppers will shop all over town at multiple stores before making their decision to purchase. At each of these stores, they ask a lot of questions, then leave. But each transactional shopper will return to only one store to make a purchase. This leaves a score of frustrated salespeople without a sale.

Meanwhile, five relational shoppers visit their favorite stores, make their purchases, and return home, accounting for a total of five store visits, five purchases, and zero frustrated salespeople.

Two Kinds of Shoppers (T) Transactional & (R) Relational

	Visit	Spend		Visit	Spend
T1	3 stores	$70	R1	1 store	$100
T2	2 stores	$80	R2	1 store	$100
T3	5 stores	$60	R3	1 store	$100
T4	3 stores	$70	R4	1 store	$90
T5	5 stores	$60	R5	1 store	$90
	18 visits	$340		5 visits	$480

Average Sale: $82 - Average Gross Profit: $32* Average Profit Margin: 39%
*Assuming a Cost of Goods Sold of $50 and a pre-discounted, original markup of 100% (Keystone)

Beware of Averages!

Only 22% of store visits (5 of 23) were made by Relational Shoppers
78% of store visits (18 of 23) were made by Transactional Shoppers

50% of buyers (5 of 10) were Relational Shoppers
50% of buyers (5 of 10) were Transactional Shoppers

59% of dollars spent ($480 of $820) were by Relational Shoppers
41% of dollars spent ($340 of $820) were by Transactional Shoppers

72% of gross profit ($230 of $320) came by Relational Shoppers
28% of gross profit ($90 of $320) came from Transactional Shoppers

But ...

10% of ad dollars were spent targeting the Relational Shopper
90% of ad dollars were spent targeting the Transactional Shopper*

The majority of all retail ad dollars are spent on "sale, price-item and event" ads that target the transactional mindset. These shoppers represent a greater share of overall store traffic than of actual sales or gross profits because they tend to visit a greater number of stores in search of the lowest price.

Two Kinds of Shoppers

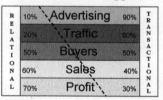

Consequently, Transactional shoppers represent *lower* closing ratios, *lower* average sales, and *smaller* profit margins.

Relational shoppers represent a smaller share of store traffic, but a *larger* share of sales, *higher* closing ratios, *higher* average sales, and *higher* profit margins.

Intentionally or unwittingly, most companies target either the transactional shopper or the Relational shopper. Who have you been targeting?

Wizard of Ads® specialize in targeting the Relational Shopper.

Information Sources Behind the
Transactional vs Relational Case Study

The terms "Transactional" and "Relational" are condensations of the highly respected research of Myers-Briggs regarding preferences among psychological types. The intent of the MBTI preference test is to reflect a habitual choice between rival alternatives. (i.e. Even though we use both the right and left hands, we will most often 'reach' with the hand we prefer. Similarly, every person uses both the transactional and relational style of shopping, but will respond first and most often with the 'preferred' attitude.)

More than 2,000,000 Americans take the Myers-Briggs test each year (www.capt.org) and based on their 30-year database, approximately 50 percent of the nation will prefer a "Transactional" style of shopping and 50 percent will favor the "Relational" method.

According to *Dr. Richard D. Grant, (*Considered one of the worlds lead - ing corporate psychologists) Transactional/Relational preferences will stem principally from the Myers-Briggs Type Indicator. T and F prefer - ences can be colored somewhat by J/P and be 'salted' a little by S/N.

The percentages used for markdowns below recommended retail in our example, are reflective of the American marketplace during the past decade. For more information, read the Business Research Yearbook edit - ed by Abbass F. Alkhafaji, Ph.D. - 1146 pages, University Press of America; (May 3, 1994) ISBN: 0819195316 or visit the Center for Applications of Psychological Type at www.capt.org.

*The figure of '90 percent of advertising' being targeted toward the trans - actional shopper is an educated guess. In reality, it may be even higher than that. Remember - more ad dollars are spent in the newspaper each year than on radio and television combined. Take a look at today's news - paper and factor all that you see, into the mix of ads that you hear on TV and radio. Then go to your mailbox and see how many pieces of junk mail arrived there today offering you a discount.

TEST THE WATERS

"Money is too precious to spend on experiments
but it's amazing how many people do."
- David Carmichael —
(Founder and CEO of the Carmichael Group of Companies, Australia)

There are approximately one hundred and twenty thousand sales people responsible for selling advertising on the television and radio stations of America and Australia. Each of these one hundred and twenty thousand sales people will make "prospecting calls" on an average of three business owners each day. One business owner out of twelve will say, "Perhaps your station is the right one for my business. I'll buy a small schedule to test the waters, and if it works, I'll start using your station on a regular basis."

Sounds reasonable, doesn't it? In reality, it's no different than standing at a roulette wheel saying, "Perhaps black is the colour for me. I'll place a small bet and if I win, I'll start betting black on a regular basis."

Thirty thousand business owners in America and Australia will decide to "test the waters" on a TV or radio station today. Most of them will experience very poor results. Will they be disappointed? Yes. Surprised? No, because most of these business owners have "tested the waters" many times before with very limited success, and the few successes they had were rarely repeatable.

Why would a business owner do what he has done before and expect a different result? It is because every one of those one hundred and twenty thousand sales people have been taught to sing a seductive little song whose chorus line is, "The secret is to reach the right people, and our people are the right people for you!" Once again, the logic of reaching the right people is extremely appealing, mostly because it's common sense. The problem is with advertising is that it so often defies common sense.

Want to hear the really sad part? Nearly every single one of the disappointed business owners would have been delighted with the station they chose had they only understood two simple laws of advertising.

Law of Advertising # 1:

It's what you say, not who you say it to, that will determine your success in advertising. Most people are "the right people," when you say the right thing! Be convincing!

Law of Advertising # 2:

Short schedules are always a gamble.
Few people will be convinced quickly, and few of those people who are convinced will have any immediate need for what you are selling. By the time their need arises, your "testing of the waters" will be over and they will have forgotten you.

You must decide what to say and then say it to as many people as you can afford to reach relentlessly. If you cannot afford to reach a station's audience with relentless repetition, you should consider buying a smaller audience. It is better to reach ten people ten times than a hundred people once.

"Testing the waters" is the signature of an uncommitted advertiser, and I've never known an advertiser to experience more than momentary success with such an outlook.

Focus and commitment are the unwavering signatures of real success. Show me an advertiser with a genuine commitment to a focused message, and I'll show you a success in the making.

"Man will occasionally stumble over the truth, but most of the time he will pick himself up and continue on."
- Winston Churchill -

"So...What Are the Secrets?"

In the consulting offices of the Wizard of Ads Partners, we are asked an amazing assortment of questions on a daily basis.

> "Which type of advertising works best?"
> "Which words are the ones people cannot resist?"
> "What type of music works best in radio ads?"
> "What color combinations have been proven to be most effective?"
> "What works best, radio, TV, or newspaper?"
> "What are the secrets? I want the secrets."

The secrets?

Here they are:
1. Decide what you have to say.
2. Find a hundred different ways to say it.
3. Say it convincingly.
4. Say it again.
5. Keep on saying it.

The effectiveness of your ad campaign will be limited only by your commitment to your message, and the persuasiveness of your ads.

How the message is delivered is completely secondary.

The secret in a phrase,

"It's what you SAY that counts."

THREE TYPES OF CUSTOMERS

Researchers from Harvard did a study on brand loyalty, revealing three types of customers:

Type 1: Non-Switchable
There is essentially nothing you can do ... or say, to cause these customers to switch from the product or service they currently use.

Maybe it's the brand of coffee you drink ... maybe it's the brand of shoes you wear ... the car you drive ... It doesn't matter. Just know that you have customer prospects out there that are **Non-Switchable**. There is nothing you can say or do to cause them to switch ...

SO DON'T LET IT DRIVE YOU CRAZY.

Type 2: Switchable
These customers may be won, but only if you say the right thing and keep on saying it until the prospect is finally convinced ... until they finally get around to giving you a try.

When you're saying the right thing, you're convincing people who are not yet in the market for your product or service, and now you have to wait until they're in the market.

Type 3: Switchable for Reasons of Price Alone
The study strongly recommended that you not pursue these customers. If you appeal to these customers, you will likely enjoy initial success, but your position will never be a strong one, because these customers will switch from you just as quickly as they switched to you and for precisely the same reason. These are the Transactional Customers.

You can never hold onto the customer who is switchable for reasons of price alone. Give 'em a lower price ... BAM! Instant Success! But you can't hang onto it! WHY? Because there's nothing in the world, that someone can't make a little worse and sell a little cheaper.

Therefore, target the switchable customer, knowing that you'll have to have patience and knowing that the longer you say the right thing ... the longer you talk to the customer in the language of the customer about what matters to the customer ... the better it's going to work.

"To excel in advertising, one must learn,
what makes people do the things they do."
- The Wizard -

How Advertising Works

1. There is no direct correspondence between dollars invested and results gained. No mathematical formula can be devised to answer the advertiser's question … "If I spend this much on advertising, what can I expect to happen?"

The amount of money you spend … and what you get for it, have virtually nothing to do with each other. Two businesses can spend an identical amount of money to reach the identical group of people; one advertiser gets rich, while the other advertiser fails miserably. So what was the difference?

2. The variable, which prohibits a mathematical formula, is the power of the message. Two advertisers can reach precisely the same audience with exactly the same repetition … one advertiser is successful, while the other fails miserably. The difference? The Message.

One advertiser spoke to customer in the language of the customer about what mattered to the customer, and the customer said YES, YES, YES, YES. The other advertiser spoke about himself, answered questions the customer wasn't asking, and the customer said, "Hey, here's 35-cents ... call your mum ... I don't care!"

The media: newspaper, TV, and radio, are not "the answer" to successful advertising. The media is purely a delivery vehicle on which your message can ride into the mind of the customer. Only after you have uncovered the correct message, determined your ad budget, chosen your strategy, and only if that strategy calls for mass media advertising, do you then choose which media vehicle is the most appropriate. Never before.

3. When a message has been uncovered which generates a positive response, a mathematical pattern does emerge. The benefit experienced in Year Two will be twice the benefit experienced in Year One, provided everything else remains equal and the core message does not change. The benefit in Year Three will be three times the benefit of Year One.

Our Wizard of Ads® clients have seen this proven over and over again in the past 16 years. **(But only after you've figured out the right thing to say.)**

As a marketing consultant, I want to uncover the right message for my client ONE time. Then we can both get lazy, knowing that this is going to take off and grow exponentially. My new challenge will then be helping my client stay on top of his growth.

At the end of about 36 months, new variables have entered the equation and now it's anyone's ballgame.

A client in Milwaukee Wisconsin has been in business for 20 years, and a Wizard of Ads® client for ten. In the past ten years, this clients company has grown to *43 times the size it was when he first got together with our firm.
(Wizard of Ads® is paid a monthly salary, reviewed each year, and increased according to the business growth … consequently, he's paying us 43 times what he paid the first year.)

Can this miraculous growth happen to all businesses? No … of course not!

The growth of your business will be determined by the following five factors

1. **Total Market Potential:** How much will be spent by the public in your product or service category this year? What is the depth of your current market penetration? How many dollars remain on the table?

2. **Message Development:** How well do you tell your story? What is the Impact Quotient of your ads?

3. **Media Plan:** How efficiently are your ad dollars being spent?

4. **Competitive Environment:** How good are your competitors at what they do?

5. **Competency:** How good are you?

Most advertisers have begun at least one great AD campaign, then "Chickened-Out."

The "chickening-out" period usually falls between the second media invoice and the third media invoice. Between week 8 and week 14.

The advertiser uncovered the right message, but didn't realize advertising has a delayed effect. It takes months, even years for the full effect of a good campaign to show results. It's like trying to push a car from a standing start. Lots of effort and strain go in at the beginning - you don't think it will move, then it moves ever so slightly. Then a little more, and soon you are trotting behind with one hand, while the car rolls along.

Little green seedlings are popping up through the soil and the advertiser says, "Yeah, I'm seeing SOME results, but not nearly enough to justify all the time and money and labor and effort we've put into it. I'm looking for a new farm."

NO, WAIT! It's about to start happening! Be patient - it's about to be payday!

We have a ritual at Wizard of Ads®. We tell new clients, "We promise you unconditionally that if we start doing the right thing, the one thing you will want more than anything 90 days from now is to fire us! We promise that you will believe it is the biggest mistake you have ever made in your life. Let's cross that bridge now."

This is BEFORE we take their money.

Let's cross that bridge now because if you don't have the courage of your convictions, if you're not totally committed to stay with this, then let's not go down this path. Half of the people who say they're ready, aren't. It's painful … it's hard.

THAT'S WHY MOST ADVERTISING IS DONE BADLY.

That's not what you really want to hear is it? But it's the TRUTH.

WHY MOST ADS DON'T WORK

Most advertising isn't working like it should. And in most instances, the blame lies entirely with the advertiser.

Most advertisers insist on repetitiously cramming the name of their company, the name of their product, their business hours, and their street address into every ad they buy. Such ads do a great job of answering the "who, what, when and where" questions while failing to answer the customer's question, **"Why?"** The simple truth is that most advertisers sound like a mob of two-year-olds in a day-care center, each one jumping and crying, "Me! Me! Me! Watch me! Look at me!"

It may hurt you to hear this, but I've got to say it anyway because I care about you: "Bad advertising is about the advertiser. Good advertising is about the customer." No, this is not just a new way of saying that you should focus your ads on the benefits of your product rather than on its features. I'm saying that you should focus your ads entirely on your *customer*. Remember: the customer isn't interested in your address or phone number until *after* you've convinced them of *why* they should care. Do your ads convincingly answer the customer's question, "Why?" or do they speak only about you, *your* products, *your* prices, *your* street address and phone number? Need an example of what I mean? Okay.

Here's a typical "advertiser focused" ad:

> "At **Used Car Warehouse**, you'll find a huge selection of clean, late model cars to fit *any* budget and *nobody* will give you more for your trade-in than **Used Car Warehouse**. Imports and locally made, sports cars and luxury cars, utes and 4wds, you're sure to find what you're looking for at **Used Car Warehouse**, open from 9 to 9, seven days a week at 210 Queens Rd. Financing available with approved credit. Call **Used Car Warehouse** at 486-757. That number again is 486-757."

Now here's a "customer focused" ad for the same advertiser:

> "From the moment you slipped the key into the ignition, you knew that *this* was *your* car. You love the way it feels on the road … in the corners … at the stoplights … Admit it; you even like the way people *turn their heads to watch* as you drive by … (Second Voice) There is *one* perfect car for every person in the world … And yours is waiting for you, *right now*, at Used Car Warehouse, 210 Queens Rd."

To make this radio script into a TV ad, all video images would need to be shot from the perspective of a driver looking out of a moving vehicle. We would show neither the vehicle nor the driver since our goal is to cause *the customer* to imagine *himself* or *herself* behind the wheel, experiencing all the things that we're describing.

Are you beginning to catch on?

"A company wearing a syndicated advertising program is like a man wearing a toupee. It's not really their own identity, but they figure it's better than not having one at all."

- The Wizard -

LET'S BEGIN AT THE BEGINNING

The Objective: To cause people to willingly take the actions you want them to take.

The Challenge: To gain and hold the attention by introducing a thought more interesting than the thought that had previously occupied the listener's mind.

The Vehicle: Intrusive, invasive sound.

The Vehicle's Fuel: Delight

Why is it that when you're driving and looking for an address, you turn down the volume on the radio? And why is it when you are watching TV and the phone rings you again turn down the volume. Ever stopped to think about it?

You can close your eyes, but you cannot close your ears. Sound is invasive, intrusive, and irresistible. You hear and retain information even when you're not listening. You hear even when you're fast asleep. How else would you know there's a burglar in the house?

One of the greatest myths in the world today is that "we remember more of what we see than what we hear." In fact, quite the opposite is true. That great scientist of the eye, Josef Albers, says it quite plainly in chapter one of his landmark book, Interaction of Color, **"the visual memory is very poor in comparison with our auditory memory."**

The primary gift of humanity is our ability to attach meanings to sounds. This is accomplished in 3 highly specialized parts of your brain - Broca's area, Wernicke's area and the Auditory Association area. *(Refer to Brain Map on page 27)* In fact, your physical ability to coordinate the movements of your diaphragm, larynx, tongue, and lips so that you can produce human speech is also owed to Broca's Area, a specialized extension of Auditory Association into the Motor Association cortex.

Did you know that the written word has no meaning until the brain has translated it into the spoken word? Ever been lying in bed reading a book and suddenly realize that you've been scanning the same paragraph over and over for a very long time and you have no idea what it says? Yes, your eyes were sending the written symbols to your brain, but those symbols were no longer being translated into the sounds they represent.

A subtle undercurrent of ongoing delight is what causes listeners to keep listening to Radio and TV ads. Delight makes Radio & TV ads magic. Predictability kills them deader than a bag of hammers. How predictable are your ads?

A great writer is one for whom writing is more difficult than it is for other people. Great writers won't allow themselves to write what comes easily, because they know that what comes easily to them will also be painfully predictable to the listener.

Clichés are easy to write because they just pop into your mind. The reason they "sound right" is because they're predictable.

There can be no delight without surprise. Surprise is the foundation of everything delightful. The amount of surprise can be as subtle as an unusual combination of words that create an intriguing mental image, or as dramatic as a great punch line. Either way, your objective is to delight the mind with the power of the unpredictable.

But is everything that is surprising delightful? Of course not! Negative surprises create confused, irritated listeners who will simply spin the dial to another station that will surprise them in happier ways.

When attempting to gain access to a listener's visuospatial sketchpad (imagination), whether in a face-to-face sales presentation or when writing a piece of Radio/TV copy, pay close attention to your action words, your verbs. Listeners can take no action they have not first imagined. To cause them to imagine an action, you must use a verb.

But NEVER the one they were expecting.

Verbs, much more effectively than nouns or adjectives, will move your message past Broca's Area, that part of the brain that rejects the mundane and ignores the predictable but allows the delightfully surprising to have immediate access to the visuospatial sketchpad of the listener's imagination. And it is on this visuospatial sketchpad that the listeners of your ads will see themselves DOING the thing you want them to do.

Whether it's a face-to-face sales presentation or piece of Radio / TV copy, the process is the precisely same. True persuasive power is always hiding in the verbs. Harness them and ride them to the top of Radio / TV Mountain.

A bad ad is about the advertiser. A good ad is about the customer.

Follow the Wizard of Ads philosophy. Apply these elements to your next commercial:

Eliminate the black words. Avoid words that do not contribute toward a more vivid or colourful mental image.

Follow the principles of Robert Frank. This writing style is accurate but selective in its inclusion of detail. It approaches a subject from an unusual angle (remember: Surprise Broca). Put the known underwater. Why state the obvious? Edit or delete information you assume the listener already knows (remember: Don't Bore Broca). Most people write about the seven-eighths already underwater. Write about the one-eighth above water.
(Robert Frank is generally regarded as one of the greatest photogra - phers the world has ever seen.)

Frosting. Replacing common, predictable phrases with unexpected, colourful ones.

Seussing. Invent words. Read a Dr. Seuss book and you will see how a man who invented words became a best-selling author.

Be Monet. In order to create great ads, follow these three rules: Ignore the details, exaggerate the colour, and remove the black.

In the same way Monet painted, write "impressionistically," rather than accurately. Use poetic exaggeration and overstatement. Select words according to the intensity of their associations, or colour. Minimize the use of black words.

Your ads must also have a **FMI**, the first mental image or opening scene, and a **LMI**, the last mental image or closing scene in a mental sequence. Great writers involve the listener as an active participant.

"A customer can do nothing that he has not "seen himself do" in his mind. The goal of advertising is to cause your customer to imagine doing the thing you want him to do. It all happens in the brain. So doesn't it make sense to know a little about how the brain functions?"

- The Wizard -

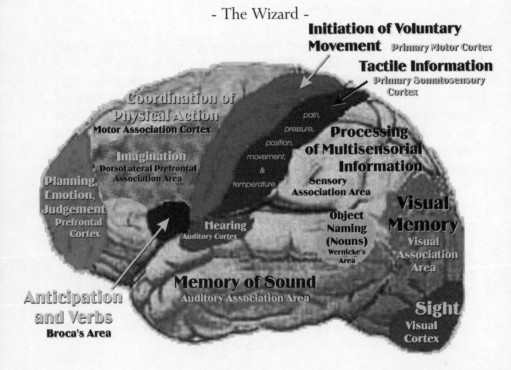

THE ADVANTAGES OF INTRUSIVE MEDIA RADIO AND TELEVISION

Echoic Intrusiveness
You can close your eyes, but you cannot close your ears. You continue to hear even when you look away.

Echoic Retention
Any competent cognitive neuroscientist will confirm that echoic memory is vastly superior to iconic memory. Words, statements, phrases, jingles, and songs, which surprise Broca's area of the brain, are much more easily implanted and recalled than visual images.

Echoic retention causes people to remember things they never committed to memory, and a working knowledge of it gives one the ability to work miracles through the power of words. **Echoic retention and the power of words is the heart and soul of advertising,** though very few ad professionals understand it.

Listener Pattern Predictability
It is easier to achieve frequency with the same listener each day on the radio than it is to repeatedly find the same viewer during television prime time. Consequently, it's much easier to win the battle of Frequency vs. Sleep using radio.

Neural Personalization of the Message
Great writers understand that the word "You" conjures up a different mental image in every human mind. One of the greatest advantages of radio is the absence of visual images. This allows the radio ad to be about the listener, personally.

Example: When you say …
"So the next time you reach into **your letterbox,**" every listener will "see" their letterbox in the **Dorsolateral Prefrontal Association Area** in their minds, their imagination. (Refer to Brain Map on previous page)

What Is "Branding," Really?

People say the word "branding" as though it's a mysterious and complex proposition. But when you peel off all the layers of hype, it comes down to this - if Advertising is "getting your name out," then Branding is simply "attaching something to your name." **A brand is simply the sum total of all the mental associations, good and bad that are triggered by a name. What does your name stand for in the mind of the public? What are the associations triggered by "(fill in your name here)?"**

The simple truth is that the advertiser's message, itself, is far more important than the vehicle of its delivery. Successful Branding depends upon your ability to speak to the customer in the language of the customer about what matters to the customer.

The goal of Branding is simply to be the name that the customer thinks of immediately, and feel best about, whenever they, or anyone who they know, needs what you sell. Branding is about the message.

Branding is far from new. Ivan Pavlov won a Nobel Prize for his research into branding in 1904. Remember the story? Day after day, Pavlov would ring a bell as he rubbed meat paste onto the tongue of a dog. The dog soon began to associate the taste of the meat with the sound of the bell until salivation became the dog's conditioned response. In psychological terms, this is known as, "the implantation of an associative memory." In other words, "branding" in all its glory.

Psychologically branding is to implant an associative memory in combination with a recall cue. What is an associative memory? An associative memory is a memory, which has become linked to another memory. Your favourite song might be linked to the night you met the love of your life. Every time you hear that song, you remember the night.

Or If I say, "It's a Steve Irwin (The Crocodile Hunter) kind of restaurant," you immediately think of the place as being, "wild, over the top, exciting, and loud" right? Your assumptions about the restaurant would be anchored to your feelings about the image of Steve Irwin.

To frequently and consistently associate the restaurant with Steve Irwin would be to implant an associative memory into the mind. Branding.

There are three keys to implanting an associative memory into the mind of the customer:

First Key: Consistency
Pavlov never offered food without ringing the bell, and he never rang the bell without offering food. In other words, Pavlov did not keep changing the campaign. He didn't say "hmmmm, maybe this here is a visual dog." He didn't say, "This ain't workin' let's try something different, the dog don't seem to get the bell thing." He knew he would have to be consistent. Never ring the bell without giving the dog meat. Never give meat without ringing the bell. He also knew he was going to have to do it frequently.

Second Key: Frequency
Pavlov did it day … after day … after day … after day.
Everybody gets Consistency and Frequency when it comes to Branding. Where they always lose out is ANCHORING.

Third Key: Anchoring
When implanting an associative memory, the recall cue (in Pavlov's case the bell) must be associated with a memory, which is already anchored in the mind. (The dog's love for the taste of meat.)

FREQUENCY AND CONSISTENCY CREATE "BRANDING" ONLY WHEN YOUR MESSAGE IS TIED TO AN ESTABLISHED EMOTIONAL ANCHOR.

Do not tie your rope to something that isn't already in the heart of the customer. Pavlov's branding campaign was anchored to the dog's love for the taste of meat. If the dog didn't love meat, the frequent and consistent ringing of the bell would have produced no response…OTHER THAN TO IRRITATE THE DOG!

The dog would have said, "I hate advertising. Would you cut it out with the bell?"

Is your recall cue, slogan, positioning statement or other repetitious element tied to an anchor in the heart of your customer? Or are you just irritating the dog? Most people are just irritating the dog...and that's why so many people say "I hate advertising." That's Broca talking. People hate BAD advertising. People hate predictable, boring, cliché advertising. But advertisers love it. They say "I'm paying for all these ads. Let's talk about me, me, me. My company. My product. My fast friendly service. People should care about ME!" Well, guess what? They DON'T!

If you desire a specific response from the buying public, you must tie your identity to an emotional anchor that's already known to elicit the desired response. If you make such an association consistently and frequently, branding will occur. But don't expect too much too soon. It takes a lot of repetition to train the public. Do you have the patience?

"If your goal is to "brand" your product, you'll need a
memorable message and sufficient weekly frequency.
Do you have them? Branding is accomplished only when you
have a salient message that is repeated with enough frequency to
become securely stored in the hard drive of the brain."
- The Wizard -

UNCOVERY

"If you're paying to advertise who you are and
you don't know who you are, you're stupid."
- Sara Boatz -
(During a discussion at Wizard Academy)

The uncovery tells how you want your business story to end, where to begin, what to leave out. It determines what you are prepared to do to achieve Success.

The Elements of an Uncovery

How Will You Measure Success?
What is it you want to happen?
What are you trying to accomplish?
What will you consider a happy- ending?
What is your destination or your ***North Star?**

The Sword in the Stone
You are searching for the story that is unique to your business. The Sword in the Stone is about the **Message**. The message you deliver to a prospective customer that distinguishes you from your competitors and makes the customer want to buy from you.

What wonderful story is yours that hasn't been told? Don't try to tell the customer your whole story; just tell your best one!

How Long is the Time Horizon?
When will success be measured?
Will you use your advertising to promote your special event or limited time offer? Or will you use advertising to become a household word?

Targeting
Do you prefer to attract Relational or Transactional customers?

Determine Your Ad Budget
Figure out exactly how much you should spend, before you pour money into advertising.

Category Dominance

The ultimate goal of branding is to establish category dominance, to be the business that customers think of immediately and the one they feel best about whenever your product category is named. Category dominance can only be achieved through focus with commitment. You must make a stand and be known for something.

What will you be known for?

Choose your Strategy - Time for *Business Topology.

Following the rules of your industry will not see any dramatic success. Rethinking the rules and introducing new concepts will push you forward to a brighter future. Having a strategy keeps all the components of your marketing working together.

What are Your Unleveraged Assets?

What do we have to work with? What hidden strengths are not being used?

Stories, Abilities, Relationships, and Products that have not previously been positioned for maximum effect.

The Media

Every media 'works' … when you know how and when to use them.
The important question is this:
"What is the highest and best use of your money?"
How efficiently are your ad dollars being spent?

An advertiser who purchases advertising on a monthly basis has no real confidence in his advertising. The greatest waste of advertising dollars and business owner's time, is booking week to week, or month to month. You do this when you have no plan for Success.

Tracking

"How are we tracking?" is the most asked question from a Wizard of Ads Partner. We ask our clients this question at every fortnightly meeting. You should ask yourself the same question. You cannot improve that which you don't measure.

WizardSword Vocabulary

- North Star -

Your North Star is the constant guiding hope that helps you choose the correct way at each turning. It will get you back on track when the waves and winds of business push you off course.

- Business Topology -

The practice of identifying *Parallel Businesses by matching their defining characteristics.

- Parallel Business -

In business topology, a "related" business which is studied in an effort to discover an innovation model.

"When you don't know where you're going,
any road will get you there."
- The Cheshire Cat -
(From Alice in Wonderland)

Media Mix

Media mix tells us that the same people, who see your newspaper ads, will hear your radio ads and notice your billboards. Media mix further assumes that the customer will recognise all these as having come from the same advertiser. Yet rarely is one of these fragmented campaigns connected in the mind of the customer.

There's a lot of truth in the religion of media mix, but it is a truth inappropriate for the small business owner.

What's good for the big corporate giants can be poison to the independent business owner.

The idea of media mix assumes that your advertising budget is adequate to do a good job in each part of the mix. Proctor & Gamble, Coke, Pepsi, Ford, and the other big boys are able to accomplish a media mix without being forced to compromise any part of it. They can mix radio, television, newspaper, magazines, and skywriting without having to do anything halfway.

Is this true of your company?

Do you have this kind of budget?

If not, I recommend that you do one thing well rather than two things badly.

"Never give up on a dream just because of the time it will take to accomplish it. The time will pass anyway."

- Earl Nightingale -

Media Dominance

The position owned by the advertiser with the greatest share of voice.

Never make the mistake of doing two things half-heartedly when you can do one thing wholeheartedly. Always dominate a medium.

If you cannot dominate all of radio, dominate a single station. If you cannot dominate a whole station, dominate a single daypart on that station. If you cannot dominate all of television, then dominate a single hour of the day. If you cannot dominate an hour, dominate a single TV show. Then when your business has grown, dominate a second and a third.

Never say, "We've already reached these people, now we need to reach some new ones." Advertising is obliterated by sleep, the great eraser of the mind. Consequently people don't stay reached anymore than the lawn stays mowed.

The key to media dominance is relentless repetition.

"There is more money wasted in advertising by underspending than by overspending. Underspending in advertising is like buying a ticket halfway to Europe."

- Morris Hite -

THE SALES REP, THE AD WRITER, AND THE BUSINESS OWNER

Though few people have ever realized it, successful advertising requires a closely-knit trio.

(1) The Media Plan or **Share of Voice* is in the hands of the advertising **sales representative**. It's the sales rep's job to deliver the greatest share of voice that the business owner's budget will allow. Beyond this, the rep can do very little.

(2) *Impact Quotient is the responsibility of **the ad writer**, the member of the team who is most often overlooked and underpaid. Without persuasive ads, share of voice is of little benefit, yet you'll often find the ad writer on the bottom of the food chain. How well do you know the person writing your ads? More important, how well does he know you?

A strong ad with a weak budget will beat a weak ad with a larger budget almost every time. So what makes more sense to you? To spend a fortune flooding the media with weak ads, or to spend a little more time raising the Impact Quotient?

(3) *Personal Experience is entirely **the business owner's** turf.
Let me say this plainly: **Advertising cannot repair a broken business. It will not make you better at what you do. It cannot turn failure into success. Advertising will only accelerate what was going to happen anyway.** Good advertising cannot be expected to erase the customer's memory of a disappointing experience or reverse the impact of a bad reputation. Conversely, the positive momentum generated by good advertising will be accelerated by a customer's happy experience. Is your company careful to deliver all that your ads promise?

Legendary ad campaigns are born in that magical instant when each member of this unlikely trio realizes that success is impossible without the best efforts of the other two.

WizardSword Vocabulary

- Share of Voice -

Your business's percentage of all the advertising done in your business category. If you advertise and your competitors do not, your share of voice is 100 percent. Share of voice can be calculated for the marketplace as a whole or for a single medium. You may have zero share of voice in one medium, but total voice in another. A greater share of voice is the result of a properly focused ad budget.

- Impact Quotient -

An ad's power to convince. Saliency or **the relevance of your message to the consumer is the single most overlooked factor in advertising today.**

- Personal Experience -

A customer's experience with your company. Your PE is effectively your reputation. The growth or decline of a business will usually follow that of the business's PE as it rises and falls. Your PE cannot be changed through advertising.

"Never be afraid to train your staff.
You may train them and they leave, but what's worse,
trained staff leaving or untrained ones staying?"
- The Wizard -

Intellect and Emotion

"Does the customer typically buy the best value, or does he buy what he **feels** to be the best value? **The truth** is that human beings usually do what their emotions dictate, then find the logic to justify it." Nothing is quite so important as **emotion** in advertising and selling. Regardless of what you sell, the important things to remember are always **the intangibles**.

As Neurologist Donald Calne puts it, the essential difference between reason (logic) and emotion is that reason leads to conclusions while emotion leads to actions.

As experts in your industry, you and your salespeople see your product far more *intellectually* than does your customer. The benefits *you* see in your product are different than the benefits *your customer* sees in your product. You see things, which make your product different from your competitor's.

Your customer sees only what your product will **do for him** and chances are, your competitor's product will do the same thing. Advertising may increase the customer's **emotional predisposition** toward your store, as well as increase the number of selling opportunities you will have, but it will always take a salesperson to close the sale.

Good advertising will begin the process of selling, but it is a process which must be completed on the sales floor. Do your salespeople know what your ads say? Are your salespeople in step with the spirit and thrust of the message you are advertising to the public?

Listening to your salespeople should be like hearing a continuation of your ads. If your advertising and your salespeople aren't saying the same thing, *you need to bring the two together*.

The most effective selling organization will be the one whose *external* sales message (advertising) is in perfect harmony with its *internal* sales message (sales presentations). If your *advertising* staff is marching to the beat of the same drummer heard by your *sales* staff, there will be synchronicity.

And **who** is that drummer your ad people and your salespeople are all straining to hear? It's **You,** of course!

CALCULATING YOUR AD BUDGET

Before you pour money into advertising,
figure out exactly how much you should spend.

The purpose of advertising is to increase the exposure of a business beyond what's provided by its physical location. An extremely high Cost of Occupancy (rent) for a landmark location is often the least expensive advertising available. Businesses who save money by investing in weak locations always have to advertise much more heavily.

While there's no "one size fits all" formula for calculating the correct advertising budget, there is a concise formula for calculating the ad budget for retail businesses and the formula can be adjusted to fit other categories.

The first thing you must do is calculate your minimum and maximum allowable ad budgets:

Step 1: Take 10 percent and 12 percent of your projected annual, gross sales and multiply each by the markup made on your average transaction. In this first step, it's important to remember that we're talking about gross markup here, not margin. Markup is gross profit above cost, expressed as a percentage of cost. Margin is gross profit expressed as a percentage of the selling price. Sell an item for $150 when it only costs you $100, and your markup is 50 percent. Your margin, however, is only 33.3 percent. This is because the same $50 gross profit represents 50 percent of your cost (markup,) but only 33.3 percent of the selling price (margin.) Most retail stores (carpet, jewelry, and so on) operate on an average markup of approximately 100 percent, some operate on as little as 50 percent markup, and others add as much as 200 percent. More expensive items, such as cars, and houses, typically carry a markup of only 10 to 15 percent.

Step 2: Deduct your annual cost of occupancy (rent) from the adjusted 10 percent of sales number and the adjusted 12 percent number.

The remaining balances represent your minimum and maximum allowable ad budgets for the year.

At this point in the calculation, you may learn that you've already spent your ad budget on expensive rent, or you might also learn that you should be doing a lot more advertising than you had previously suspected.

Now let's calculate an ad budget. Assume that my business is projected to do $1 million in sales this year, I have a profit margin of 48 percent, and my rent is $36,000 per year. The first thing to do is calculate 10 percent of sales and 12 percent of sales ($100,000 and $120,000, respectively).

Second, we must convert my 48 percent profit margin into markup, because markup is what we've got to have to make this formula work. Most business owners know their margin by heart, but never their markup. To make the conversion from margin to markup, simply divide gross profits by cost. Dividing $480,000 (gross profits) by $520,000 (hard cost) shows us that a 48 percent margin represents a markup of 92.3 percent. Bingo.

Now we multiply $100,000 times 92.3 percent to see that our adjusted low budget for total cost of exposure is $92,300. Likewise, we multiply $120,000 times 92.3 percent to get an adjusted high budget for total cost of exposure of $110,760. From each of these two budgets, we must now deduct our $36,000 rent. This leaves us with a correctly calculated ad budget that ranges from $56,300 on the low side to a maximum of $74,760 on the high side.

Most advertising salespeople will tell you that "5 to 7 percent of gross sales" is the correct amount to budget for advertising, but don't you believe it. It simply isn't possible to designate a percentage of gross sales for advertising without taking into consideration the markup on your average sale and your rent. Yes, expensive rent for a high-visibility location is often the best advertising your money can buy, since a business with a good sign in a high-visibility location will need to advertise significantly less than a similar business in an affordable location. To prove this, just look at the example above and change the rent to $75,000 per year. In this case, the ad budget would range from $17,300 to $35,760, representing just 1.7 to 3.5 percent of sales.

The formula I've given you is the only one that reconciles your ad budget with your rent as well as the profitability of your average sale.

Good luck!

Example

Total Annual Sales	$1,000,000
	x 10%
Budget for <u>TOTAL Cost of Exposure</u> (Cost of Occupancy plus Advertising)	$100,000
Average Markup	x 92.3%
Adjusted Budget for **Total Cost of Exposure**	$92,300
Cost of Occupancy	- 36,000
AD BUDGET	$56,300

**Visit www.WizardofAds.com
for your free Ad Budget Calculator**

"Every business owner must decide for themselves what percentage of
their profits to take out of their company and how much to re-invest in
their facilities, equipment, advertising and people.
Sadly, due to the near-universal fear that "If it doesn't work, I've wasted
my money," very few business people are willing to
advertise as aggressively as they should.
**Consequently, unrestrained growth is available in most categories
to those who can afford the dollars and stomach the risk."**
- The Wizard -

THE TOP 12 ADVERTISING MISTAKES TO AVOID

Spending all your money on advertising but getting no results?
Find out whether you're guilty of committing one of these huge blunders.

1. The Desire for Instant Gratification

Most advertisers like to believe that advertising is like a bubble-gum machine. You put your money in, turn the handle, and out come the results.

IT'S NOT LIKE THAT!

The decision a person makes today is very rarely influenced by the ads she heard today, this week, or even this month. **You can attract the transactional customer that way, but the longer you keep doing what works immediately, the less and less well it will work.**

It's a law of the universe. It's true in agriculture, it's true in physics, it's true in chemistry, and it's true in advertising.

Ask your Doctor how to feel good, and he'll look you squarely in the eye and say, "Eat right and exercise." Yet for every dollar spent in fitness centres, people spend nineteen dollars on cocaine. The reason? Two seconds after you snort cocaine you feel like Superman. Two weeks of diet and exercise just makes you sore and hungry.

The desire for instant gratification is harmless enough if the only thing it leads you to do is pay higher prices at a convenience store. But heaven help you if you demand instant gratification from your advertising! The businessperson looking for a financial quick fix will soon discover the cocaine of advertising, a four-letter magic chant:

Sale! Sale! Sale!

Good advertising is painful at first because you don't see immediate results. The impatient business owner will usually snort a little ad cocaine and then get defensive about it: "How can this be bad for me? I've never done better!"

But just as the junkie never stops to consider how the drug is destroying his physical health, the business-owner never stops to consider how "Sale! Sale! Sale!" undermines his business health. The first dose of ad cocaine makes him feel great. So does the next, and the next, and the next – though it takes larger and larger doses to get the same effect. Therefore, it's almost impossible to convince the addict he has a problem, even though he started with only "Twenty Percent Off" and has now progressed to "Half Price."

Successful companies don't spend their ad dollars training their customers to wait for a sale.

Do you?

Price Promotions

Summary of a report from the *Research & Development Initiative*.

Does your organization spend a lot of resources on price promotions? The latest price promotion report discusses the effects of price promotions on a product's long-term sales and profit potential.

In brief, price promotions:
1. **Do not attract new customers**
2. **Do not lead to extra subsequent sales**
3. **Do not affect repeat buying loyalty**
4. **Do not reach many customers.**

HOWEVER, price promotions do produce up and down sales blips at a great cost.

Professor Andrew Ehrenberg, Professor of Marketing at South Bank University, London created the R&D Initiative in 1997; prior to this Ehrenberg spent more than 20 years as Professor at London Business School.

*This report was also published in 1994, **Journal of Advertising Research**, 34, July-August, pp. 11-21. "The After-effect of Price-related Consumer Promotions,"*

by Ehrenberg, A, Hammond, K and Goodhardt, G.J

Now I have warned you about the insidious nature of Ad Cocaine, here's how to make it.

Creating a short-term successful hype ad is simple.

Here's all you need:
1. **Intrusiveness.** You've got to get their attention.
2. **Offer.** Make it too good to pass up.
3. **Logic.** Add supporting evidence to make doubters believe.
4. **Urgency.** There's got to be a time limit.
Plus
5. **Frequency.** Lots and lots of frequency.

Leave out any of these ingredients, and you're dead in the water.

The trouble is with Ad Cocaine the advertiser becomes instantly addicted. But the Law of the Universe says, "Anything that works quickly will work less and less well the longer you keep doing it. The magic always fades. Sadly, like all addicts, these advertisers resist taking the long-term view, and they continue to measure success on an extremely short time horizon.

Mitigating Cocaine's Danger

Have you shouted "Sale!" so often that customers now ask your salespeople, "When will this go on sale?" Do you find it more and more difficult to sell products that aren't on sale? Do you have a business cocaine habit you would like to kick, but worry about the financial withdrawal pains?

Do you remember the 3 types of customers mentioned at the start of the guide?

You'd like to begin branding your name in the better customer's long-term (chemical) memory instead of depending on a series of short-term (electrical memory) promotions targeted to the switchable for-reasons-of-price-alone customer. But you're afraid to quit the short-term gimmicks because you're worried that you won't be able to survive the chickening-out period between seedtime and harvest, right?

Another thing that worries you is how long it's been since you met anyone willing to pay full price. Down deep, you worry that all customers are coupon-clipping, grave-robbing, bargain-hunting predators who will never agree to buy from you unless they're convinced they're getting "the deal of a lifetime."

Bottom line: You have a history of attracting customers for reasons of price alone. So how can you now begin attracting better customers without losing the coupon-clipping grave robbers too soon?

Answer: Use a visual recall cue in a non-intrusive (silent) medium. Run a newspaper ad with a large picture of what's "On Sale!" but with your company's name buried in the fine print. The only people who will know it's your company having a sale will be those looking for your product.

The newspaper's lack of intrusiveness, its principal weakness in long-term branding, now lets you advertise your Hurry! Hurry! Once in a Lifetime Sale "anonymously."

Humans don't see unless they're looking. The only people to notice the visual recall cue, the photo of your product, will be those looking to buy your product. But humans hear and retain information even when they are not listening, so above all, DO NOT use TV, or radio ads to stimulate response to the newspaper ad. Unless, of course, you want to train everyone who is not now in the market to wait for your next sale.

During this newspaper-advertised "sale," allow your broadcast ads to continue building long-term brand awareness in the minds of the not yet in the market majority.

The downsides of this technique:

1. You can't get away with it forever if you keep it up, and soon you'll be right back where you started.

2. Because you will be maintaining two separate ad campaigns, your advertising costs will be way out of line throughout the three to six month period of transition.

3. It isn't painless and easy - it's painful and hard - because sometimes the

newspaper ads don't pull.

But if you're truly committed to taking your company in a new direction, you will survive this difficult transition period and emerge from it more profitable, with more consistent customer traffic patterns and more stability throughout your customer base.

Good luck.

And remember: One day at a time.

ELB'S

Exponential Little Bits... tiny but relentless changes that compound to make a miracle. The power of an ELB lies not in its size, but in its daily occurrence. For an ELB to work its Exponential magic, the Little Bit must happen every day... every day... every day. Every day. Funny thing... When daily progress meets with progress, it doesn't add, **it multiplies**.

- The Wizard -

2. Attempting to Reach More People than the Budget Will Allow

Advertising schedules should be proposed and considered according to their reach and frequency. That's how advertising works!

Reach (the total number of people who will hear your message)
&
Frequency (the number of times they hear it)

Think about it this way: Would you rather reach 100% of the people and convince them 10% of the way of them, or reach 10% of the people and convince all of them all the way? The advertising cost is the same.

Most advertisers reach too many people with too little repetition. If they would only reach fewer people with sufficient repetition. How much repetition is sufficient?

The average message must be received by the identical individual 3 times in 7 nights sleep.

If you cannot afford sufficient repetition during prime time, buy off-prime. Why? Because sleep erases advertising. Reach fewer people, but reach them more often.

How many people can I afford to reach?

There are two critical ratios here....
(1) How many dollars do you have to spend?
(2) What is the cost of advertising in your marketplace?

Am I willing to give you a rule of thumb? Yes, but it's a dangerous rule of thumb.

The **average business owner** who is focused, and has a long-term plan, can reach a person for about 2 dollars, 3 times a week, 52 weeks a year.

Two dollars per person, per year.

If you have a $40,000 ad budget, you can dominate about 20,000 people. That's whether you're in a town of 40,000 or a town of 4 million. You have about a 20,000-person ad budget. Don't try to reach 100,000 people.

Most advertisers are reaching too many people with too little repetition. As a result, the only people they're reaching effectively are the people that just accidentally happen to be in the market for this product right now. They don't have enough repetition to build ongoing brand awareness.

If you're going to try to win the heart of the customer before they need what you sell, you have to reach them repetitiously and patiently wait for them to be in the market for what you sell.

What is "word-of-mouth" advertising? It is the result of somebody having been impressed deeply. How are people impressed deeply? You're good at what you do and they actually experienced it -OR- you said something very memorable - something that surprised the hell out of Broca. **Saliency** is what neurologists call it - you probably know it better as **Relevancy**. If the saliency or relevancy was high in the message, it was memorable. And they heard it enough times to go from short-term electrical memory to long-term, or chemical, memory. But you still need the frequency because of SLEEP, the great eraser of advertising **that** MUST BE DEFEATED.

Successful advertising is the result of good writing and strong frequency.

Are you buying too much reach and too little frequency with your ad budget? Have you bought into the myth of "media mix"? Are your ads underproducing due to fragmented placement and poor scheduling?

By simply rearranging your current media schedules, you could dramatically increase the effectiveness of your ad budget.

3. Assuming the Business Owner Knows Best

The business owner is uniquely unqualified to see his company or product objectively. Too much product knowledge leads him to answer questions no one is asking. He's on the inside looking out, trying to describe himself to a person on the outside looking in. It's hard to read the label when you're inside the bottle.

Sometimes it helps to bring in an objective outsider to give you some perspective.

4. Unsubstantiated Claims

Advertisers often claim to have what the customer wants, such as "highest quality at the lowest price," but fail to offer any evidence. An unsubstantiated claim is nothing more than a cliché the prospect is tired of hearing. You must prove what you say in every ad. Do your ads give the prospect new information? Do they provide a new perspective? If not, prepare to be disappointed with the results.

5. Improper Use of Passive Media

Nonintrusive media, such as newspapers and yellow pages, tend to reach only buyers who are looking for the product. They are poor at reaching prospects before their need arises, so they're not much use for creating a predisposition toward your company. The patient, consistent use of intrusive media, such as radio and TV, will win the hearts of relational customers long before they're in the market for your product.

6. Creating Ads Instead of Campaigns

It is foolish to believe a single ad can ever tell the entire story. The most effective, persuasive, and memorable ads are those most like a rhinoceros: They make a single point, powerfully. An advertiser with 17 different things to say should commit to a campaign of at least 17 different ads, repeating each ad enough to stick in the prospect's mind.

7. Obedience to Unwritten Rules

For some insane reason, advertisers want their ads to look and sound like ads. Why?

8. Late-Week Schedules

Advertisers justify their obsession with Thursday and Friday advertising by saying "We need to reach the customer just before she goes shopping." Why do these advertisers choose to compete for the customer's attention each Thursday and Friday when they could have a nice, quiet chat all alone with her on Sunday, Monday and Tuesday?

Memory is formed from images, but not of the images we have seen with our eyes. Memory is formed from the images we have seen in the imagination. **For your ads to be effective, they must be recalled when the prospective customer has need of what you've advertised. Do you know how to make your ads memorable, or are you foolishly attempting to schedule your ads to the precise moment of the customer's need?**

Tell the customer WHY and wait for WHEN.
Quit trying to predict his moment of need.

9. Over-Targeting

It's a myth that you only need to get your message to the decision-makers. In truth, decisions are seldom made in a vacuum.

Each of you has a realm of association of approximately 250 coworkers, friends and family ... people you play golf with … parents of children who play basketball or football with your kids ... you go to church with them ... you live in their neighborhood … you work with them ... or they're your blood relatives.

Now, if I could only afford to reach 10 percent of your community, and I needed to reach you, but you weren't part of the 10% I was reaching, I wouldn't worry about that. Because I've still reached 25 of your best friends.

I'm not going to target more people than I can afford to own. I'm going to say something memorable ... I'm going to say something persuasive ... and pretty soon ...

Wizard of Ads does not ALLOW our clients to reach more than 50% of their market. We have a number of advertisers right now whose revenues and budgets have grown so that they could reach literally more than 50% of their market 3 times a week, 52 weeks a year, and no matter how much bigger the business gets we say, "Trust us. The half we're reaching now already knows the other half."

Many advertisers and media professionals grossly overestimate the importance of audience quality. In reality, saying the wrong thing has killed far more ad campaigns than reaching the wrong people. It's amazing how many people become "the right people" when you're saying the right thing.

The true secret of advertising success is to say the right thing to as many people as you can afford to reach over and over. Word-of-mouth advertising is the result of having impressed someone, anyone, deeply.

10. Event-Driven Marketing or Expiration-dated advertising

For each of our senses, the brain offers short-term and long-term memory. Short-term memory is electrical. Long-term memory is chemical.

The objective of "branding" is to cause your product to be the one the customer thinks of first and feels the best about when their moment of need arises. Consequently, branding must be accomplished in long-term memory. No problem, it's just a matter of repetition, right? Wrong. The brain, you see, is a very smart organ. It knows better than to transfer information into long-term memory when that information is flashing a "soon-to-expire" message in neon letters.

I'm referring to ads that make a limited-time offer. When an advertiser insists on trying to "whip people into action" with the urgency of a limited-time offer, they can be sure that their message will never make it into long-term memory. At best, the message will stay in short-term memory only until the expiration date has passed and then it will be forever erased from the brain.

Yes, limited-time offers, when they work, cause people to take action immediately. The downside is that limited-time offers don't work better and better as time goes by. In truth, they work worse and worse. When an advertiser makes a limited-time offer, the only thing that goes into long-term memory is, "this advertiser makes limited-time offers." In essence, the advertiser is training the customer to ask, "When does this go on sale?"

Consequently, you cannot use a series of limited-time offers as the foundation for a long-term branding campaign.

A special event should be judged only by its ability to help you more clearly define your market position and substantiate your claims. If 1 percent of the people who hear your ad for a special event choose to come, you will be in desperate need of a traffic cop and a bus to shuttle people from distant parking lots. Yet your real investment will be in the 99 percent who did not come! What did your ad say to them?

11. Great Production without Great Copy

Too many ads today are creative without being persuasive. Slick, clever, funny, creative and different are poor substitutes for informative, believable, memorable and persuasive.

12. Confusing Response with Results

The goal of advertising is to create a clear awareness of your company and its unique strength. Unfortunately, most advertisers evaluate their ads by the comments they hear from the people around them. The slickest, cleverest, funniest, most creative and most distinctive ads are the ones most likely to generate these comments. See the problem? When we confuse response with results, we create attention-getting ads that say absolutely nothing.

Wizard of Ads partner clients measure the results of their advertising success by growth in sales volume, not by comments from friends.

Radio Scheduling

For which of the following do you plan to use radio?
   1. Draw a crowd to a special event or sale
   2. Make the name of your business a household word

Short Term – Special Events and Sales

Special Events

To advertise a special event on radio, (like a concert) you should schedule an ad to air just before the event begins, then move backward in time, scheduling one spot per hour until you have run out of ad budget. Generally, a special event schedule should be at least thirteen spots per day, 6am – 7pm,* for at least five days prior to the event. *If you have the available budget, add a spot an hour during the evening and overnight hours for a total of 24 spots per day per station.

Sixty-five spots should be considered an absolute minimum schedule on each of the stations you plan to use.

(If you can persuade a station's General Manager to let you air two spots per hour, then schedule two spots per hour. The goal is to increase the ratio of ad repetition to listener sleep.)

Sales

The same applies for a sale, only you start the first ad a few hours before the end of the sale.

Example, you are having a three-day sale starting on Friday morning, ending Sunday afternoon at 5pm. Your first ad should run about 2pm or 3pm on Sunday afternoon. Then work back an ad an hour between 6am – 7pm for at least sixty-five spots per station or until your budget runs out.

Always remember, sleep is the great eraser of electrical memory. As the mind is purged each night, the memories that are the most quickly and completely erased are those that are no longer relevant. No ad with a deadline is relevant after the deadline has passed.

Long Term – To Make your Business Name a Household Word

The real power of radio, however, is long-term memory, or "top of mind awareness." **Smart advertisers are those who set out to win the customer's heart long before she needs their product. Their only goal is to be the company she thinks of first and feels the best about whenever her need arises. Smart advertisers make no attempt to predict the moment of the customer's need but they buy enough repetition to ensure their company will immediately spring to mind whenever such need arises.**

To become a household word, you must buy at least twenty-one radio ads per week (plus or minus two ads), per station, 6am to 7pm, fifty-two weeks per year, on as many stations as you can afford. Plan to endure minimal results during the first eight to fourteen weeks of your schedule. This is know as the "chickening-out period," when you will probably spend a lot more on radio advertising than you will see in results.

Establishing Echoic Retention:
Variables are
1. Power of the message (emotional voltage)
2. Repetition (frequency)
3. Consistency

When you have a commitment to a 52-week consistency and an average message, a 3 frequency can be established with nearly two-thirds of the weekly cume on most radio stations with 21 ads per week (plus or minus two ads), 6am -7pm.

Across Australia, commercial radio is consumed regularly by about 76 percent of the adult population of any town.

As a rough rule of thumb, if you have a big enough ad budget to buy all the radio stations in your market, with a 3 frequency or approximately 21 ads per week, 6am to 7pm, you will reach just on 50 percent of the population of your market.

Critical Equation: The ratio of ad repetition to listeners sleep.
Assuming an average message, the individual listener needs to hear the identical ad 3 times within each 7 night's sleep.

Sleep erases advertising.

Variables: The formula assumes that the message is of average impact and that the majority of the audience is not currently in the market for the product. Other variables are the number of years of repetition and the strength of the competitors.

Change your ad when the listener has been exposed to the identical information 12-20 times.

Horizontal Scheduling
When faced with too large a station and too small a budget, consider buying a "station within the station." Example: Schedule 21 spots per week, fifty-two weeks per year, between the hours of 7pm and midnight, and you will typically reach less than half the station's weekly audience, but you will have good repetition with the segment you're reaching. The schedule will also be dramatically less expensive than a comparable daytime schedule.

Vertical Scheduling
Another successful scheduling technique is to buy a "vertical" schedule on Sundays, airing one spot per hour for at least 13 consecutive hours, fifty-two weeks a year. Though radio listenership is somewhat lower on Sundays than weekdays, rates sometimes can be bought at a less expensive rate. Like the 7pm to midnight schedule discussed above, the vertical Sunday schedule gives you a "station within a station" and allows for solid repetition with at least a certain percentage of the station's total audience. (Our firm has often bought late nights and Sundays only.)

Word of mouth advertising is created when people talk about things that have impressed them deeply – whether positive or negative. Are you impressing the public with ads that have impact and meaning? Are you impressing your customers with the world inside your door?

Television Scheduling

Like radio the real power of television, is long-term memory, or "top of mind awareness.

In television, you generally get what you pay for. However, there are a couple of mistakes you definitely don't want to make.

1. Never buy run of station.
TV stations will offer dramatically reduced rates in return for the freedom to place your ads within broad windows in their daily schedules. Though the rates may look attractive, such schedules make it virtually impossible to reach viewers with enough repetition to be effective. The greatest likelihood is that you will reach an enormous number of different people approximately one time each. Although it's possible to see results using run of station, it's never the highest or best use of your money.

2. Don't assume the viewer is loyal to a particular station.
Although television viewers may have loyalty to a particular TV show, they rarely have loyalty to the station. Even when viewers are loyal to a particular news show, it's the show to which they are responding, not the station. It's a tragic mistake to believe that a particular station's audience is intrinsically different from the audience of another. The show is what attracts birds of a feather, not the station.

There are three things to remember when placing a television schedule:

1. Always schedule horizontally.
The best way to ensure that you'll reach the same person with a second and third repetition of your ad is to buy advertising in the same television show over and over again.

When booking long-term, look for programs like the news, the soaps, programs that run 5 times a week, 52 weeks a year. Book **at least** 1 ad per day, 5 days per week, 52 weeks a year.

2. "Roadblock" when your ads have a high impact quotient.

When your ad is irresistible and you need to make sure that you're reaching the largest number of people that you possibly can, try roadblocking at a particular time each day – buy fixed position ads to air simultaneously on every station in town. (A viewer might run from your roadblock, but he can't hide.)

3. Find a sales rep who will keep your best interests in mind.

Things change quickly in television, and a sales rep who's watching out for you is worth her weight in gold.

"So which kind of advertising will you do?

Short-term or long-term?

Will you have a little piece of cake right now, or a series of larger pieces later on? This is the choice every advertiser makes, either consciously or unconsciously. I want you to make it consciously."

- The Wizard -

How's Your Gravity Well?

Sales trainers who focus on "closing the sale" assume that the relationship between seller and buyer is adversarial, rather than one of mutual good. As a result, the selling style they teach is often offensive and demeaning, a canned series of loaded "trick 'um and stick 'um" questions designed to hustle the buyer into whatever the salesperson wants to sell. Is it any wonder that a mother never says of her little boy, "I hope he grows up to be a salesman?"

Great sales trainers teach that a salesperson should aspire only to become the customer's servant, consultant, and friend; and having accomplished this, never to violate the terms of that friendship.

Human persuasion is not a confrontation with each side trying to "win."

What a business wants is a committed customer. But a customer is far more likely to make a small commitment, or to increase an existing commitment by a small degree, than to make a large commitment abruptly. Commitment is rarely an all-at-once thing. Salespeople who ask for large commitments too soon are typically referred to as "Pushy," and most people hate dealing with them.

Profitable persuasion and comfortable customer compliance are merely the result of a properly constructed gravity well. Have you ever charted your own gravity well?

A properly constructed gravity well softly pulls, entices, and seduces the customer into gradually deeper and deeper degrees of commitment. But unlike the tricky "sales trap," the customer may comfortably exit the gravity well at any time.

Shaped like a funnel, the gravity well is most easily entered at the uppermost level, and requires only the mildest level of interest. In this, the widest part of the funnel, your customers will be numerous but uncommitted.

Just inside the rim of Wizard of Ads Australia's gravity well is the *Monday Morning Memo*, written by Roy H. Williams. The *MMM* is a weekly newsletter sent at no charge to subscribers around the world.

Next is the free Wizard E-book *Making Ads Work*, available for download at WizardofAds.com & WizardAcademyPress.com. Making Ads Work is also available in print.

Those who wish to delve deeper will buy one or more of our other books, an investment of tens of dollars.

A large number will attend a *Wizard of Ads* seminar. This could be either paid, or as the guest of a media network.

Many will attend a *Making Ads Work* one-on-one teaching session for a few hundred dollars. This is an extension of the book where a Wizard Partner will go into more depth on the subjects and questions of **your** choosing. This session is available in person or by phone.

At the next level, readers may opt to purchase one of our video series, like *Secret Formulas School of Advertising,* a twelve-session video library.

Next, business owners may spend just under one thousand dollars to attend a personal half day consulting session. This is where we can review their current advertising, brainstorm, or discuss possible business ideas.

Some may consider flying to Austin Texas, to attend a *3-day Magical Worlds Academy, the Wizard of Web Academy, Create a Cult Brand, or one of the other courses taught at Wizard Academy Home Office.

*The 3-day Magical Worlds Academy, in Austin Texas, normally priced at $3,500 is offered at no charge for Partner Clients of Wizard of Ads. (Airfares, accommodation and transportation not included.)

Finally, from the very tip of the funnel will trickle the occasional new ***Partner Client** who asks to pay our firm thousands of dollars per year in return for creating and guiding his ad campaign.

*A Partner Client is a client who has undergone an Uncovery with a Wizard Team and then hires that team on a monthly basis (12-month agreements) to guide their advertising campaign.

But at no time in the process is anyone asked to buy anything. That's the elegance of a gravity well. Sales resistance is what happens when the customer is asked to jump too deeply into the well, too quickly.

So how's your gravity well?

Can you list the steps your prospective customers need to make?

"The best time to plant a tree was 20 years ago.
The second best time is today."

- Gerry Harvieux -

WHEN GOOD ADS FAIL

A Monday Morning Memo Example

You ran an inspired series of wonderful ads. And got nothing in return. What?

Like so many Sir Galahads on the quest for the Holy Grail, businesspeople continue to search with near-religious ardor for "the perfect ad campaign." And many, when they have found it, learn that it's not enough.

One of the greatest myths in marketing is the belief that advertising, by itself, is able to drive steady traffic into a business. This perception is supremely evident when a businessperson looks at an ad professional and says, "My only problem is traffic. If I had more traffic I'd sell more customers. Traffic is your department. Bring me customers. Now."

What makes good ads fail?

1. Too Little Repetition

If your ad doesn't make an irresistible, limited-time offer, you're going to have to run it often enough for customers to first become aware of it, and then to become familiar with it. Next, you've got to wait for them to need what you sell. And the longer the product-purchase* cycle, the longer you may have to wait. (*Restaurants will see results more quickly than carpet stores because we eat more often than we replace our carpet.) Ads that make an irresistible, limited-time offer may work like magic, but the longer you run them; the less well they work. Until they finally quit working altogether. So what do you do then?

2. Deeply Entrenched Competitors

No matter how good your ad campaign, it may not be enough to take customers away from a competitor who's doing a good job of meeting their needs. Many businesspeople have failed simply because they picked the wrong towns in which to open their businesses. Eighty miles away, the same efforts may have made them kings and queens of all they surveyed; but in the towns they chose, they got squashed like bugs. When you see a mountain that's being guarded by a giant who never sleeps, it might make sense to pick another mountain on which to plant your flag.

3. Failing to Deliver

Face it. Directly or indirectly, every ad is a promise to the customer. And the more powerful the ad, the bigger the promise implied.

How many disappointed customers does it take before the whole town has heard that you don't deliver what you promise? For your ad campaign to work in the long run, you must deliver to your customer exactly the experience that was promised in your ads.

4. Lack of Interest

As unbelievable as this may sound, not every business is commercially viable. Sometimes, regardless of how wonderful its advertising, a business is simply answering a question that no one was asking. In these instances, the failure wasn't in the ads, but in the business model.

Are you avoiding these four mistakes?

Roy H. Williams

Subscribe to the free weekly Monday Morning Memo at
www.WizardofAds.com

"Sadder than living your whole life without ever achieving
your dream would be to live your life without dreaming.
But perhaps the greatest tragedy of all would be to have a dream
and achieve it, never realizing that happiness is
not the reward at the summit of the climb.
Happiness is the climb."

- Roy H. Williams -

An Advertiser's Question

A Monday Morning Memo Example
(Abbreviated from the original)

Q: I'm a 52-week radio advertiser currently reaching 32% of my area's 18-34 population with a frequency of 2.9 each week, 52 weeks in a row. (I know you teach that weekly frequency should be at least 3.0, but I figured 2.9 was close enough.) Today I have a very specific question, which no one can answer, so I'm writing to you. Here it is: "How much will my store traffic increase if I increase my spending to <u>reach</u> 48% of the population with similar weekly <u>frequency?</u> How many more sales will I make?"

A: Your question is far more complex than you realize, but I will do my best to answer it: "All things being equal, increasing your reach from 32% to 48% (an increase of exactly 50%,) should increase your ADVERTISING DRIVEN traffic by exactly 50%." And I agree that a weekly frequency of 2.9 is "close enough" if you are achieving it 52 weeks out of 52.

Now for the problems:

1. "All things" are never equal. My answer assumes there will be no change in the number of competitors in your marketplace or in the attractiveness or aggressiveness of existing competitors - yet rarely do these remain static. If your competitors drop the ball, you may experience a significant increase in traffic without increasing your ad budget at all. Likewise, if your "share of voice" increase is matched by similar increases from your competitors, your increase will be effectively nullified and store traffic will remain at current levels.

But what if they increase their ad spending and you don't increase yours? You want to do the math on that one?

2. What percentage of your traffic is currently "advertising driven"? What percentage is location driven? What percentage are repeat customers? What percentage are referrals? A 50% increase in reach (without a decline in frequency) should increase your ADVERTISING DRIVEN TRAFFIC by 50%. But can you tell me how much of your traffic is due to advertising alone and would not be coming to you otherwise?

Are you beginning to understand why it would be completely irresponsible of me to predict the bottom-line impact of an increase in advertising?

But this is my day to be irresponsible, so here's my answer:
My instinct is that 50 to 70 percent of the typical retailer's store traffic is due to location, signage, repeat customers, referrals, etc., and the remaining 30 to 50 percent of store traffic is advertising driven.

This would mean that a 50% increase in effective reach should increase traffic by 15 to 25%.

Roy H. Williams

"Your customer will buy whichever product he
"feels best" about.
Let's make sure he feels best about **yours**."
- The Wizard -

QUESTIONS FOR YOU

"As I continue in this business, (Advertising) I realize that
clients do not want to know much about what they are buying.
Worse, they will take ads and plans presented to them and
retool them to their own tastes and vision—
most of which is frighteningly off-base.
They want magic beans and a big beanstalk overnight."
- Brett Feinstein -
(Partner - Pound, Feinstein & Associates, Inc.)

Each business is unique, just as each market is unique. Therefore, there is
no "one size fits all" marketing or advertising plan. You cannot simply
copy an ad that has worked for another business and expect it to work for
you.

The heart and soul of your advertising should be everything that is uniquely and wonderfully **you**. Your company is much bigger and much more
wonderful than price and item advertising. So put some effort into digging
for the diamond. When you uncover the real you, you'll have a treasure
no competitor can steal.

At the beginning of this guide you determined how much of your current
advertising is wasted. You now know how advertising *really* works. You
have learned the principles of how the Wizard Partners grow their clients
not just by percentages but by Multiples.

So what are you going to do differently?

Are you willing to take responsibility for your advertising success?

Will you book long-term or short-term?

Will you target Transactional or Relational shoppers?

Will you focus your ad budget and own a smaller group of people or will
you try to reach everyone?

Will you dominate a media or spread your dollars everywhere?

Will you invest in the advantages of intrusive media (Radio and TV) with its power of echoic retention? Or will you spend your money in passive media? (Newspaper and Yellow Pages)

Will your business be the one potential customers think of first, and feel best about whenever they or any of their friends have a need for your product or service? Or will you train your customers to wait until your next sale?

The principles in this guide are the result of proven scientific research, sixteen years of documented client growth, plus a few hundred million dollars of actual invested advertising dollars.

So do you have the commitment and courage to follow the Wizard of Ads principles? Or will you continue to test the waters, doing the same thing and hoping for a different result?

Will you run with the big dogs? Or will you stay on the porch?

The choice is yours.

"One should never attempt to launch a revolution with people who are contented with the status quo. Failure awaits any writer who attempts to create an exciting ad campaign for a company that is not committed to change."

- The Wizard -

Who Becomes a Wizard Client?

It all starts with a smart client. Bad business operators will lead to bad results. We cannot help an advertiser who is not delivering a positive experience to the customer. Ultimately, the advertiser must be good at what they do, or there is no advertising plan in the world that can help them.

So, how do we determine who deserves to be a Partner Client of Wizard of Ads? We ask ourselves, do we really believe in this business? If so, why?

It requires a subjective judgment, but there's really no other way. The most trustworthy indicator of potential success is passion. As our prospects talk about their company — its goals, products, history — we look for the gleam in their eyes and listen for the commitment in their voices.

The Asked or Often Unspoken Question

"If I hire Wizard of Ads, what am I going to get for my money?"

The answer: What **are** you getting for your money?

The amount of money you have budgeted for your advertising has already been determined. What are you getting for your money? You're spending it already. What return on that investment are you getting?

Not hiring us is much more expensive than hiring us!

Ultimately, the return on your advertising investment is determined by two things:

What is the impact quotient of your message
How compelling…How memorable…How sticky is your message?

How efficiently are your dollars being spent?

What are you getting for your money?

We spend your dollars more efficiently and put together a more effective media plan so that you reach more people. Then, we compound it by reaching these people with greater repetition, and compound *that* by giving you a more memorable and compelling message.

If you believe you are getting maximum return on your advertising investment today, then don't consider hiring Wizard of Ads. But if you are unsatisfied with what you are getting for your money, let us show you how we can do more with your ad budget than anyone else in the world.

Wizard of Ads Fees

This is where Wizard of Ads is different from most advertising agencies and consulting firms. Our income isn't tied to your ad budget. Our annual salary is tied to your growth. **When we take on a new client we always say, "In a few years if you are not prepared to pay us 5 times, 10 times what you will pay us in the first year, please do not become a client of Wizard of Ads.** We charge less at the start than our services are worth; it is not until years 3 or 4 that we start earning what we are worth. We look for little companies that are doing everything right (except marketing and advertising), and have the potential to become big companies. So we only take on clients who want a long-term business relationship.

We Do Not Pursue Clients

Relationships that are hotly pursued and entered into with great fanfare seldom turn out to be good ones. This is precisely why Wizard of Ads Partners never actively pursues a prospective client, regardless of how attractive that client may appear. We believe in courtship, in getting to know one another, in seeing our partner "real". We want to plug into the long-term hopes and dreams of our client/partners. We want to know exactly why we're running the race together. We need to see and understand the prize at the finish line.

We elect not to "pursue" business because long-term relationships seldom form between the hunter and the hunted. Real partnership is never the result of sharing a short-term objective.

Relationship, partnership, and deep commitment are the result of sharing a dream that is profoundly meaningful to both parties.

The Wizard of Ads firm is hired by clients to fill the role of marketing consultant. For us, this means telling a client the truth even if it hurts. If you want sugarcoated answers to your problems … if you want yes-men … don't hire a Wizard of Ads partner.

The functions a Wizard of Ads team performs for our partner clients…

1. Uncovery
2. Marketing and Advertising Strategies
3. Message Development
4. Media Planning

The last piece of the advertising success and business growth puzzle is

5. A Good Business

As a marketing consultant, I can help and guide you with the first four. But I'm relying on you for number five.

If you'd like to discuss adding your company to the growing list of thriving businesses being guided by a Wizard of Ads branch office, please call or email. You'll be glad you did.

"It's a wise man who profits by his own experience, but it's a good deal wiser one who lets the rattlesnake bite the other fellow."

- Josh Billings -

Craig Arthur
Managing Partner
Wizard of Ads (Australia)

Making Ads Work - One on One Training
(For Business Owners & Advertising Professionals)

Half Day Consultations
Business Uncoveries
Long-Term Marketing Partnerships
(Marketing Strategies, Message Development, Media Planning)

Speaking*
(*Tailored Marketing and Advertising Presentations)

Ph 07 47284866
Fax 07 47284868
CraigArthur@WizardofAds.com

PO Box 984, Townsville, 4810, Australia

In North America
Call or Email
Wizard of Ads Co-ordinator

Corrine Taylor

US Toll Free 800.425.4769
International 512.295.5700
Corrine@WizardofAds.com

The End?

No, you have just begun to climb!
Good luck, and remember, one day at a time.

WHO IS THE WIZARD?

Writing:
His books and Monday Morning Memos are a constant source of fascination and entertainment for his students and friends around the globe. His first book, **The Wizard of Ads,** was voted Business Book of the Year in 1998. His second book, **Secret Formulas of the Wizard of Ads**, was named the Wall Street Journal's number one Business Book in America in 1999 and became a New York Times bestseller. The third book in the trilogy, **Magical Worlds of the Wizard of Ads** reached bestseller status again in late 2001. His fascinating fourth book, **Accidental Magic**, is a tightly condensed anthology of writing tips and insights, mixed with artistic examples provided by 106 of his amazing protégés. The Wizard's first fiction book, **Free the Beagle** released October 18, 2002 is a powerful allegory aimed directly at the heart of the reader

Speaking:
More than 130 universities in the US and abroad have heard Roy H. Williams present his thought provoking seminars on marketing and advertising.

Once introduced as "the most magnetic and mesmerizing speaker in the world today," the Wizard has been trying to live up to those words ever since. Most attendees agree that his action-packed seminar, *"**Advertising in America: What Works, What Doesn't and Why**" is perhaps the most entertaining and enlightening 3 hours they have ever experienced. The seminar begins with a detailed look at the architecture of the human brain, followed by the "Four Tugs-of-War," "What is Branding, Really?" and "The 12 Most Common Mistakes in Advertising.

"What ever your event requirements may be, the Wizard can tailor his presentation to fit the specific needs of your audience. The Wizard's speaking fee in the US and Canada is currently $20,000 (US dollars) plus airfare, provided that the trip not require him to spend more than one night away from home ($50,000 US dollars plus airfares for overseas engagements).

For more information email **Corrine@WizardofAds.com**
or call Corrine Taylor at (800) 425-4769 or (512) 295-5700

*Procter & Gamble, the Direct Marketing Association, Clear Channel Communications, J. Walter Thompson have paid tens of thousands of dollars to hear Roy H Williams present **Advertising in America: What Works, What Doesn't and Why.**

Teaching:
The brainchild of his wife, Pennie Williams, Wizard Academy was founded as a way to get her husband off the road. "Instead of sending him to them for a few hours, why not let them all come here for a few days?" But not even Princess Pennie knew how well her idea would work. Since its launch in May of 2000, Wizard Academy has attracted a roster of students that includes many of the world's most forward-thinking and successful CEOs, educators, journalists, inventors and consultants. The Wizard Academy reunion each autumn is an event not to be missed.

Publishing:
Created to be a publishing springboard to showcase the work of Wizard Academy students, **Wizard Academy Press** publishes primarily audio books with accompanying transcripts.

Consulting:
For those wishing to have the Wizard review their advertising, help them plan an ad campaign, brainstorm with him, discuss a business possibility or bounce an idea off him, we've made a very limited number of days available in Austin each month at $5,000/day (US dollars).
For more information email **corrine@wizardacdemy.com** or call Corrine Taylor at (800) 425-4769 or (512) 295-5700

CEO:
A lifelong student of humanity, Roy H. Williams has spent a quarter-century asking, "What makes people do the things they do?" And he's been using the things he's learned to stimulate miraculous growth for his small business clients for more than 16 years.

("Small business clients" are defined as owner-operated businesses with sales volumes between one million and twenty million dollars a year. Clients with sales volumes larger than twenty million dollars have typically grown by percentages rather than by multiples. Their growth could not, therefore, be
conscientiously described as "miraculous.")

With ten branch offices in the US, Canada, and Australia, Roy Williams and the Wizard of Ads Partners, are now serving the advertising and marketing needs of business owners around the globe.

The Wizard of Ads Partners:
Ranging in age from 23 to 48 years old, the Wizard of Ads team combines the imagination of youth with the wisdom of experience. Partners are not assigned to clients according to geographic proximity, but a specialized team is assembled by matching partner talent and experience to fit each client's specific needs. As a Wizard of Ads client, you will have at least 2 professionals assigned to your account, each of whom will have access to the intellectual firepower of the complete partner base. In other words, each team in the field is backed up by wondrous depth on the bench.

Questions about Wizard of Ads in Canada and the United States
Call Corrine Taylor at 800.425.4769 or 512.295.5700
or email Corrine@WizardofAds.com

Questions about Wizard Academy?
Email: Info@WizardAcademy.com

Want to Find Out More about the Wizard?
Operations manager Corrine Taylor knows all there is to know.
Email Corrine@WizardofAds.com

A Closing Thought
What do Rich People have in Common?

Okay then, besides having a lot of money, what do rich people have in common?

No, it's not intelligence or education. Look around. The world is littered with unrewarded geniuses and every store has at least one clerk with a master's degree or a doctorate.

No, it's not conservatism, courage, luck or wealthy families. And no, it's not even passion, instinct, timing or greed.

The single characteristic that rich people tend to have in common is an unusually long time horizon.

In other words, rich people get rich because they think further ahead than the rest of us. As a matter of fact, research indicates that the length of your time horizon is the one characteristic that most accurately predicts where you will land in the socioeconomic strata.

Ask him how he chooses investment properties and George Stakis, the renowned multimillionaire real estate magnate, will tell you, "There's one question that I ask myself when looking at a property, even if I plan to own it for only a few hours... 'Is this a property that I would want to own 20 years from today?' If the answer is 'no,' then I don't buy it."

Wealthy people routinely plant seeds that won't bear fruit for months or even years. But counter to what you may be thinking, wealthy people don't share this characteristic "because they're rich and can afford to think ahead." They become wealthy because they have this characteristic.

The average person thinks ahead exactly one paycheck. We know what must be paid with the one that's coming and we have a plan for what to pay with the next. Needless to say, this is not a plan for building wealth. This is a plan for being average.

How far have you been thinking ahead? (It's never too late to change.)

THE WIZARD

WEBSITES TO VISIT

Subscribe to the free Monday Morning Memo at **www.WizardofAds.com**

www.WizardofAds.com	Home of the Wizard Partners
www.WizardAcademy.com	Want to change the world?
www.WizardAcademyPress.com	Do you have a book in you?
www.EmployeeSpotLight.com	Customer Service by Craig Arthur
www.FreetheBeagle.com	Do you know the way to Destinae?
www.FutureNowInc.com	Want to maximize your online marketing?
www.InvisibleHeroes.com	Heroes whose tales were never told

BOOKS TO READ

The Wizard of Ads – *By Roy H. Williams*
(Turning Words into Magic and Dreamers into Millionaires)

Secret Formulas of the Wizard of Ads - *By Roy H. Williams*

Magical Worlds of the Wizard of Ads – *By Roy H. Williams*
(Tools and Techniques for Profitable Persuasion)

Accidental Magic – *By Roy H. Williams & The Graduates of Wizard Academy*
(The Wizards Techniques for Writing Words Worth a Thousand Pictures)

The Power of Cult Branding – *By BJ Bueno*
(How 9 Magnetic Brands Turned Customers into Loyal Followers – and Yours Can Too!)

Take Your Words to the Bank – *By Bryan Eisenberg, Lisa T. Davis, & Jeffery Eisenberg*
(The Marketer's Handbook of Persuasive Online Copywriting)

Free the Beagle Trilogy – *By Roy H. Williams*

The Natural Advantages of Women – *Audio Book By Michele Miller*

VIDEOS & DVD'S TO WATCH

Secret Formulas School of Advertising – *By Roy H. Williams*

Synergistic Co-Workers - *By Dr. Richard Grant*

The 10 Most Common Mistakes in Public Relations – *By Dean Rotbart*

The Right Stuff for Radio Sales Success – *By Chuck Mefford*

The 12 Most Common Mistakes in Advertising – *By Roy H. Williams*

All the above and much, much more are available at
www.WizardAcademyPress.com